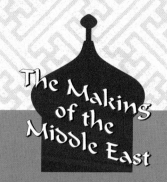

The Making of the Middle East

The
Arabian Peninsula
in the Age of Oil

The Making
of the
Middle East

The Arabian Peninsula in the Age of Oil

John Calvert

Mason Crest Publishers
Philadelphia

Frontis: Oil blows from a well tapped at Dammam, Saudi Arabia, during the 1930s. The discovery of oil had a transformative effect on the Arabian Peninsula.

Produced by OTTN Publishing, Stockton, N.J.

Mason Crest Publishers
370 Reed Road
Broomall, PA 19008
www.masoncrest.com

First printing

1 3 5 7 9 8 6 4 2

Library of Congress Cataloging-in-Publication Data

Calvert, John.
    The Arabian Peninsula in the age of oil / John Calvert.
        p. cm. — (The making of the Middle East)
    Includes bibliographical references and index.
    ISBN-13: 978-1-4222-0172-5
    ISBN-10: 1-4222-0172-4
    1. Arabian Peninsula—History—Juvenile literature. 2. Saudi Arabia—History—1932–   —Juvenile literature. 3. Petroleum industry and trade—Arabian Peninsula—History—Juvenile literature. 4. Persian Gulf War, 1991—Juvenile literature. I. Title.
    DS244.512.C35 2007
    953.05—dc22
                                                2007024590

Table of Contents

Introduction:
The Importance of the Middle East

The region known as the Middle East has a significant impact on world affairs. The countries of the greater Middle East—the Arab states of the Arabian Peninsula, Eastern Mediterranean, and North Africa, along with Israel, Turkey, Iran, and Afghanistan—possess a large portion of the world's oil, a valuable commodity that is the key to modern economies. The region also gave birth to three of the world's major faiths: Judaism, Christianity, and Islam.

In recent years it has become obvious that events in the Middle East affect the security and prosperity of the rest of the world. But although such issues as the wars in Iraq and Afghanistan, the floundering Israeli-Palestinian peace process, and the struggles within countries like Lebanon and Sudan are often in the news, few Americans understand the turbulent history of this region.

Human civilization in the Middle East dates back more than 8,000 years, but in many cases the modern conflicts and issues in the region can be attributed to events and decisions made during the past 150 years. In particular, after World War I ended in 1918, the victorious Allies—especially France and Great Britain—redrew the map of the Middle East, creating a number of new countries, such as Iraq, Jordan, and Syria. Other states, such as Egypt and Iran, were dominated by foreign powers until after the Second World War. Many of the Middle Eastern countries did not become independent until the 1960s or 1970s. Political and economic developments in the Middle Eastern states over the past four decades have shaped the region's direction and led to today's headlines.

The purpose of the MAKING OF THE MIDDLE EAST series is to nurture a better understanding of this critical region, by providing the basic history along

with explanation and analysis of trends, decisions, and events. Books will examine important movements in the Middle East, such as the development of nationalism in the 1880s and the rise of Islamism from the 1970s to the present day.

The 10 volumes in the MAKING OF THE MIDDLE EAST series are written in clear, accessible prose and are illustrated with numerous historical photos and maps. The series should spark students' interest, providing future decision-makers with a solid foundation for understanding an area of critical importance to the United States and the world.

(Opposite) This colored drawing of a caravan traveling along the Gulf of Aqaba, the western coast of the Arabian Peninsula, was made in 1839. (Right) Arabs pose outside their sheikh's desert fortress, circa 1890. Tribal groups such as this one often held power over small areas of the peninsula.

1 *Arabia in the 1800s*

*T*he modern history of the Arabian Peninsula begins in the 18th century. At that time Arabia was a relatively undeveloped region with a population of perhaps one million people. The relatively small population was largely the consequence of Arabia's harsh and inhospitable landscape.

Most of the peninsula is desert, and agriculture depended on the availability of underground water resources. Much of the settled agriculture was concentrated in two mountainous regions, Oman and Yemen; Yemen's agriculture benefited from the twice-yearly monsoon rains that swept in from the Indian Ocean. Several important settlements could be found in the interior of Arabia. Among them were Hail and Dariyya in Nejd, Rustaq in Oman, and Sana in Yemen. However, the most important towns were situated on the coasts; these included Kuwait, Muscat, Aden, Hudayda, and Jedda. Outside of the towns, a significant portion of the population was pastoral, depending on flocks of sheep and goats. Industry in Arabia was rudimentary and consisted mainly of pearling and shipbuilding along the Persian Gulf. In the Shammar Mountains in the north of the peninsula the Arabs bred horses, which were exported through the ports of Kuwait and Qatif to British India where there existed a market for fine horses. During the 1860s and 1870s horses competed with dates for the distinction of being Arabia's top export. The *hajj*, the great pilgrimage to Mecca, employed many local Arabs each year.

During this period, no sense of national identity existed among the inhabitants of the Arabian Peninsula. In fact, Arabian politics would not be affected by nationalism until well into the twentieth century. Instead, Arabians considered themselves primarily as members of clans and tribes. This was the case with sedentary as well as nomadic groups, although tribal bonds were somewhat less important in the towns and oasis settlements. Tribes provided individuals with protection against enemies. Those who stood outside of the tribal framework, such as foreign merchants and slaves, relied on the good will of particular tribes for their security. Each tribe had its leading clan, from which was selected a sheikh, or leader. Tribes made alliances with one another but such alliances tended to be temporary.

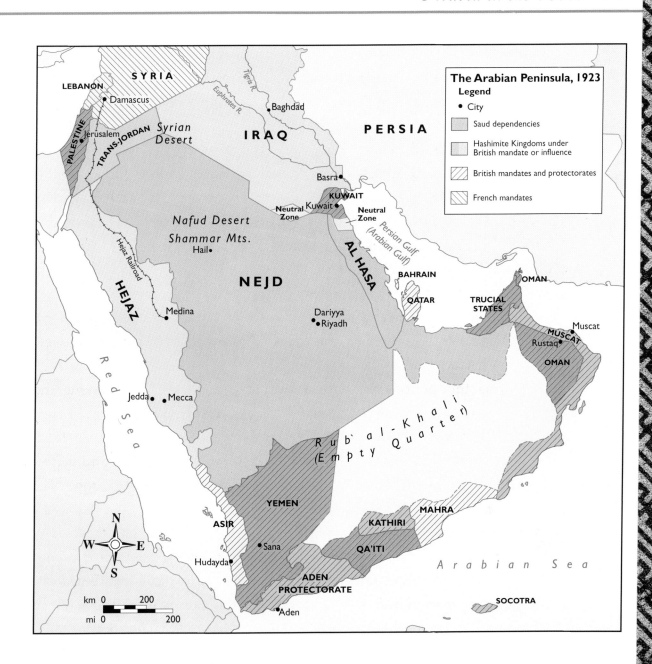

The Arabian Peninsula, 1923
Legend
- City
  - Saud dependencies
  - Hashimite Kingdoms under British mandate or influence
  - British mandates and protectorates
  - French mandates

SYRIA
LEBANON
Damascus
PALESTINE
Jerusalem
TRANS-JORDAN
Syrian Desert
IRAQ
Baghdad
Euphrates R.
Tigris R.
PERSIA
Basra
KUWAIT
Kuwait
Neutral Zone
Neutral Zone
Persian Gulf (Arabian Gulf)
BAHRAIN
QATAR
AL HASA
OMAN
TRUCIAL STATES
Muscat
MUSCAT
Rustaq
OMAN
Nafud Desert
Shammar Mts.
Hail
NEJD
HEJAZ
Hejaz Railroad
Medina
Dariyya
Riyadh
Red Sea
Jedda
Mecca
Rub' al-Khali (Empty Quarter)
MAHRA
KATHIRI
QA'ITI
YEMEN
ASIR
Sana
Hudayda
ADEN PROTECTORATE
Aden
Arabian Sea
SOCOTRA
N W E S
km 0 200
mi 0 200

A Muslim prays in the Masjid al-Haram, a revered mosque in Mecca. Daily prayer is one of the five main requirements of Islam, as is the duty of each Muslim to make a ritual pilgrimage (*hajj*) to Mecca at least once in his or her lifetime if physically and financially able to do so.

Religious Influences

One thing that all of the Arab tribes shared was religious beliefs. Practically all of the people of the Arabian Peninsula followed Islam, the religion established there in the seventh century by the Prophet Muhammad. All Muslims share certain beliefs and practices, known as the Five Pillars of Islam. These include a profession of faith (*shahada*), daily prayer (*salat*), charitable giving (*zakat*), fasting during the month of Ramadan (*sawm*), and the requirement of making a pilgrimage to Mecca (*hajj*). The sayyids—descendants of the Prophet Muhammad—played an important role in Arabia as the mediators of tribal disputes, and were valued for their knowledge, religious status, and tribal neutrality.

There are two main divisions within Islam, as a result of a schism over leadership of the faith that occurred in the late seventh century. Sunni Muslims are the larger of the two groups, making up about 85 percent of the total Muslim population worldwide. Sunnis follow the teachings of the Qur'an, the holy scripture of Islam, and the example of the Prophet Muhammad as laid out in the *hadith* (reports of what the Prophet said and did). Although the Shiites, the smaller group, also revere these sources, they have additional traditions and beliefs, such as the veneration of the Imams, the religious and political leaders of the Shiites, which differ from those of the mainstream Sunnis.

In the 18th century, the overwhelming majority of Arabs in the Arabian Peninsula were Sunni Muslims; this was true, for example, of the Qawasim and Banu Yas tribes, which lived in small settlements on the shores of the Gulf. However, a significant population of Shiites existed in Kuwait and Bahrain and in the al-Hasa region in northeast Arabia. In addition, there was another Shiite sect in Yemen and a large community of Ibadi Muslims in Oman.

The Ibadis were a Muslim group that evolved from a seventh-century Islamic sect called the Kharijis. Although Ibadis are similar to to Sunnis in terms of belief and practice, they nevertheless maintained a religious identity distinct from other communities of Muslims. Under the leadership of the Bu Said dynasty, Oman's Ibadis established a large trading empire in the Indian Ocean region that included Zanzibar and other East African towns.

Other religious minorities in Arabia included an ancient community of Jews in Yemen, and Hindu merchants who were scattered along the Gulf coast. Historically, relations among these various religious communities were peaceful and were upset only by the advent of the Saudi-led Wahhabi movement in the eighteenth century.

Ottoman Involvement in Arabia

During the 18th and 19th centuries, two outside powers, the Ottoman Empire and Great Britain, exercised various degrees of authority over the coasts and the interior of Arabia. However, the overall influence of these powers over Arabian affairs was limited. The Ottoman Empire, which had risen to prominence in the 14th and 15th centuries, was the most powerful Muslim state in the world during the 18th century. From its capital at Istanbul, the empire administered Slavs and Greeks in the Balkans; Turks, Kurds, and Christian Armenians in Anatolia; and Arabs in North Africa, the Levant, and the Arabian Peninsula. However, the Ottomans' grip on their remote Arabian provinces was tenuous and in certain places in the Peninsula, non-existent. Since the 1500s the Ottomans had held no effective power along the Gulf coast and in the interior of Arabia. By the early 18th century the Ottomans had lost control of Yemen, Aden, and Hadramaut to local rulers. In addition, although the Sharifs of Mecca acknowledged Ottoman supremacy, in fact they governed the region of the western

Arabian Peninsula along the Red Sea, known as the Hejaz, as independent rulers.

In the 19th century the Ottomans made several attempts to regain control of Arabia, but these efforts ended mostly in failure. In one of these campaigns the Ottomans fought to recover control of Yemen's interior. Stiff resistance on the part of the Yemenis prompted the Ottomans to concede independence to the highland regions of the country in 1911.

At the same time the Ottomans attempted to impose their control over the holy cities of Mecca and Medina. As part of this effort, the Ottomans constructed the Hejaz Railway, which linked Damascus and Medina. The railway was built to help Muslim pilgrims travel to Mecca, but it could also be used to facilitate the movement of Ottoman troops into Western Arabia. However, as in Yemen, the Ottomans did not succeed in bringing the region firmly under their control. The Ottomans' only clear success was in al-Hasa, where they forged an alliance with the Rashidi family, which ruled the city of Hail. But even in this case success was short-lived: The alliance did not survive the coming to power of another Arab family, the Saudis, in al-Hasa after 1902.

A station on the Hejaz Railway, which was constructed between 1903 and 1908. Although the stated purpose of the railroad was to enable Muslim pilgrims to reach the holy cities of Mecca and Medina more easily, Ottoman rulers intended the rail line to bind the Hejaz closer to their empire by making it easier to move Turkish troops into the Arabian Peninsula.

The feelings of Arabs toward Ottoman rule was dramatically manifested in the Arab Revolt of 1916–1918, during which Bedouin forces from Western Arabia attacked the local Ottoman garrisons with British assistance. Ottoman ambitions in Arabia ended with the defeat of the empire by Britain and its allies during World War I. Following the war, the victorious allies dismembered the empire and set the stage for the emergence of new states.

British Involvement in Arabia

British interest in Arabia stemmed from the need to protect imperial communications with its colony in India. The British viewed the piracy and maritime warfare of the Gulf Arabs as potentially dangerous to British interests. The British were also worried about Ottoman influence in an area so close to the Suez Canal—Britain's lifeline to its worldwide empire. In an effort to keep peace along the Gulf, Britain persuaded the ruling sheikhs of the principal tribes living along its southern shore, including those of Abu Dhabi, Sharja, Dubai, Ajman, and Umm al-Quwayn, to observe a truce among themselves during the months when pearl fishing took place. Britain took responsibility for enforcing the truce, agreeing to maintain maritime peace in the Gulf and preserve the independence of the sheikhdoms, which became known as the Trucial States. The truce was extended in stages until 1853 when it was made permanent. In 1861 the island sheikhdom of Bahrain was brought into the agreement.

Britain did not want other powers to gain a foothold in the region, so in the 1880s and 1890s Bahrain and the Trucial sheikhdoms signed further agreements that required them to place the conduct of their foreign relations in British hands and not to give up to others any part of their territories without British permission. In 1899 the emir of Kuwait, Mubarak al-Sabah, fearful of Ottoman attempts to seize his territory, signed a protectorate treaty with Britain. The Sultan of Oman entered into a treaty of friendship with Britain in 1908, while Qatar was brought into the trucial system during World War I. Although the presence of the Ottomans and Iran prevented the Gulf from being exclusively a British preserve, by the late 19th century Britain was the predominant power in the region.

Britain also held a dominant position along the coast of southern Arabia, starting with its acquisition of the port of Aden in 1839. Aden was important to the British as a coaling station for ships on the Bombay-Suez route and as a bastion to guard against potential Ottoman expansion in the Red Sea. For nearly a century Aden was administered from India as an outpost of Britain's Indian empire. However, in 1937 Britain separated Aden from the Indian administration and made it a crown colony directly administered by the British government in London.

Beginning in 1873 Britain expanded its zone of influence in southern Arabia by signing treaties with some 23 sultanates and emirates in south Yemen and Hadramaut. In basic form, Britain's various arrangements with the sheikhdoms and emirates of the Gulf and the Red Sea held until the 1960s.

Religious Revival in Arabia

The most consequential development in Arabia during the 18th and 19th centuries was the rise to power of the Wahhabi-oriented Saudi family. The theological foundations of the Wahhabi movement were set by a religious scholar from Nejd, the central region of Arabia, named Muhammad ibn Abd al-Wahhab (1703–1792). The son of a *qadi*, or religious judge, Abd al-Wahhab received his education in Mecca, Medina, and Basra (in what is now Iraq). He followed the Hanbali School of Islamic law and was influenced by the 13th-century theologian Ibn Taymiyya. As a serious student of the Qur'an and other Islamic sciences, Abd al-Wahhab was appalled by the superstitions and religious practices that had crept into Islam in Arabia over the centuries. He was particularly angered at the people's practice of seeking the intercession of dead holy men at shrines erected over their graves. In the view of Abd al-Wahhab, this "cult of saints," which was widespread throughout the Islamic world at that time, was a form of polytheism that compromised *tawhid*, the essential monotheistic nature of Allah (God).

For the same reason Abd al-Wahhab condemned the devotion of Shia Muslims to their imams—the descendants of Ali, the Prophet Muhammad's cousin and son-in-law, and Muhammad's daughter Fatima. In the view of the Twelver Shia, the imams possessed both religious and political authority. Whereas the Shia regarded pilgrimages to the tomb-shrines of the imams as acts of devotion, for Abd al-Wahhab such acts were idolatry. In his view, whoever sought the help of any being but God was an unbeliever who should be fought until he came to worship God alone.

Abd al-Wahhab's strict fundamentalism was at odds with the spirit of tolerance that had generally prevailed in Islamic lands throughout history. However, in the view of his followers, his teaching represented nothing less than the revival of authentic Islam after centuries of decadence. The nascent movement did not call themselves "Wahhabis," for to do so would have glorified Abd al-Wahhab at God's expense. Rather, they called themselves al-Muwahhidun, "those who affirm the unity of God." Although this latter term continues to be used by the adherents of this particular understanding of Islam, some Muslims today prefer the term "Salafi," referring to the pure belief and practice of the *salaf*, companions of the Prophet who led exemplary lives. (Outside of the modern state of Saudi Arabia, most people refer to Abd al-Wahhab's reform movement as Wahhabism, however.)

Abd al-Wahhab's preaching attracted the support of a local chieftain from Nejd, Muhammad ibn Saud. With the conversion of ibn Saud to the Wahhabi cause, Wahhabism became the religious ideology of tribal unification. Echoing the life of the Prophet, ibn Saud waged war against the tribes in Nejd and converted them to the reformed version of Islam. Undoubtedly, many peninsular Arabs were as much attracted to the booty that came to them as participants in ibn Saud's jihad as they were to Abd al-Wahhab's teachings. Jihad legitimized the accumulation of wealth on behalf of a political center and a ruling family, and made possible the creation of a simple Saudi state. In contrast to other Islamic reform movements in the 18th and 19th centuries, the Wahhabi-Saudi jihad was not a response to Western imperialism but rather a reaction to developments that had taken place within Islam.

The Rise of the House of Saud

Muhammad ibn Saud died in 1765 and was succeeded by his son Abd al-Aziz (1721–1803) who continued the conquests. In 1773 Abd al-Aziz's forces captured the small city of Diriyah and made it their capital. In 1802 they

Remains of an ancient mud brick fortress at Diriyah, near the modern city of Riyadh. It was from his stronghold at Diriyah that Muhammad ibn Saud and his descendants gained control of Nejd.

mounted a great raid against Karbala in Ottoman Mesopotamia, where they destroyed the shrine-tomb of Hussein ibn Ali, the most venerated of the Shia Imams after the Prophet Muhammad's cousin and son-in-law, Ali ibn Talib. The following year Abd al-Aziz was assassinated in Diriyah by a Shiite who wished to avenge the sack of Karbala. He was succeeded by his son, Saud ibn Saud (1748–1814) who continued his father's militant policy. In 1810 the Saudis raided as far as the outskirts of Damascus, Syria. By the early years of the 19th century, the Saudis controlled most of the Arabian Peninsula, including the Hejaz and parts of Oman and Yemen.

The Ottoman sultan, Mahmud II, was concerned about Saudi incursions into territories claimed by the empire, especially the Hejaz. As protector of the two holy sanctuaries, the sultan was responsible for ensuring the safety of Muslim pilgrims and therefore could not tolerate the capture of Mecca and Medina by Saudi militants. Moreover, he believed that the Saudi movement's fundamentalism upset the tolerance for religious diversity that had been a characteristic of the Ottoman Empire. He therefore ordered Muhammad Ali, his representative in Egypt, to mount an expedition to destroy the power of the Saudis in Arabia. Muhammad Ali delegated the task to his sons, Tusun and Ibrahim; the latter succeeded in 1818 in defeating the Saudis and capturing the Saudi ruler Abdullah, who had taken power after the death of Saud ibn Saud. Ibrahim sent the defeated Saudi ruler to Istanbul, where he was paraded through the streets and beheaded. Over the next two decades Muhammad Ali appointed a series of governors to rule over Arabia and the severely diminished Saudis. However, the Ottoman occupation of Nejd, Hejaz, and al-Hasa came to an end in 1840 when a British threat to Egypt prompted Muhammad Ali to withdraw his troops.

During the middle decades of the 19th century the Saudi house survived as a small tribal principality in the interior of Arabia. In the 1860s a succession dispute weakened the house further. The Al Rashid, whose power base was the Shammar Mountains in northern Nejd and its capital Hail, took advantage of the Saudis' disarray. The Rashidis enjoyed a reputation in Arabia of being fierce and proud warriors. Having been conquered by the Saudis in the 1810s, they desired revenge. Attracting Shammar tribes to their cause, the Al Rashid began expanding their territory north and south. After taking Riyadh, the Al Rashid decisively defeated the Saudi forces at the Battle of al-Mulayda in 1891. With the defeat, Saudi power in Arabia was at its lowest ebb in over a century.

Abd al-Aziz ibn Saud (opposite) emerged as ruler of much of the Arabian Peninsula after a power struggle with the Sharif of Mecca, Hussein ibn Ali (right, center wearing white turban). During the mid-1920s Abd al-Aziz defeated the Hashemite forces and established the state that would become Saudi Arabia.

2 The Creation of Saudi Arabia

The Saudis of Riyadh chafed under Rashidi rule. The Saudis regarded the Rashidis as pawns of the Turks and as favoring the Shammar tribes over the local Wahhabi population. Taking advantage of the confused situation that followed the death in 1897 of the Rashidi emir Muhammad ibn Rashid, the Saudis began to reassert themselves. In 1902 Abd al-Aziz ibn Saud, son of the Saudi leader, mounted a daring raid against Rashidi-held Riyadh. With only 60 men Abd al-Aziz succeeded in capturing the city. In campaigns over the following years he continued to fight the

Rashidis and their Ottoman allies. Abd al-Aziz decisively defeated the Rashidis in the early 1920s.

Upon taking control of territory, Abd al-Aziz followed the practice of previous Saudi regimes of sending religious scholars (*ulama*) to the towns and the villages to instruct the population on the beliefs of Wahhabi Islam. Wherever they could, the Saudis destroyed tombs and shrines, enforced public prayer and the separation of men and women, and outlawed the consumption of alcohol and tobacco.

The Birth of the Saudi Kingdom

During World War I Britain gained the cooperation of Abd al-Aziz against the Ottomans by recognizing him as sovereign over the territories he had conquered in Arabia, and by granting him subsidies and weapons with which to fight the Rashidis and their Ottoman allies. At the same time, Britain encouraged Abd al-Aziz to cooperate with Sharif Hussein, the Hashemite emir of Mecca who launched the Arab Revolt in 1916. However, the two Arabian rulers viewed each other with growing hostility. Abd al-Aziz regarded Sharif Hussein as an emerging rival who aimed to extend the Hashemite domain into Nejd at the expense of the Saudis. For his part, the sharif was suspicious of his rival's ambitions in the Hejaz. Moreover, he viewed Abd al-Aziz as a rough barbarian. Although both the Saudis and Hashemites attacked Ottoman forces in Arabia, they did so without receiving aid from the other.

Abd al-Aziz's military strength rested on the Ikhwan, or "brethren," an army of Bedouin devoted to the Wahhabi creed. They replaced the farmers and

Bedouin soldiers gather in a small village in the Jordan Valley during a World War I campaign. The Arabs launched their celebrated revolt against Ottoman rule with the expectation that the Allies would grant them independence once the war ended. These hopes were dashed at the 1919 Paris Peace Conference, when Arab territories were divided into new states (Syria, Iraq, and Transjordan) and placed under the control of Britain and France.

townspeople who had previously constituted the main coercive force at the disposal of the Saudis. Abd al-Aziz's broad purpose in creating the Ikhwan was to direct the raiding instincts of the Bedouin away from intertribal warfare and toward state-sponsored jihad. He understood that the tribes' blood feuds and rivalries drained the Saudi movement of common purpose. In order to dampen the Bedouin habit of raiding, he settled the Ikhwan in agricultural communities, which, he hoped, would eliminate their desire to attack other tribes for booty. In addition, he made sure that the Ikhwan received portions of the spoils of war won by the House of Saud in the course of its struggle against regional enemies. Through these means, he created an attack force relevant to the centralizing purposes of the developing Saudi state.

At the conclusion of the war tensions between Sharif Hussein and Abd al-Aziz flared. At the Paris Peace Conference that ended World War I, the British had arranged for the installment of the sharif's sons, Abdullah and Faysal, as rulers of Transjordan and Iraq, two new states created from the Ottoman territories and placed under British control by the League of Nations. Abd al-Aziz viewed this development as leading to Hashemite encirclement. Further, he was concerned that Hussein's status within Arabia and his legitimacy in the wider Islamic world were rising. Hussein, who had assumed kingship over the Hejaz in 1916, claimed the title of caliph just days after the new government of Turkey, which had replaced the Ottoman Empire, abolished the caliphate in 1924.

In a bid to destroy his rival, Abd al-Aziz led his Ikhwan troops against Hussein's Hashemite forces in 1924. Britain, which, during the war, had poured money and weapons into the Hashemite Arab Revolt, failed to come to Hussein's assistance. After Abd al-Aziz seized Taif, Mecca, and Medina, Hussein abdicated and went into exile. Thereafter, all of the Hejaz fell easily into Saudi hands.

Britain responded to the new situation by signing the Treaty of Jedda in 1927, which recognized Abd al-Aziz as sultan of Nejd and king of Hejaz. In return, Abd al-Aziz acknowledged Britain's special treaty relationships with the emirates of the Gulf and pledged not to interfere in their affairs. By that time other countries, including the Soviet Union, had recognized Saudi sovereignty over the territories claimed by Abd Al-Aziz. On September 18, 1932 Abd al-Aziz officially merged Nejd and Hejaz and formed the Kingdom of Saudi Arabia. The robust warrior-chieftain from Nejd was now the ruler of a new, independent state.

The Structure of Politics in Saudi Arabia

Over the following decades Abd al-Aziz ibn Saud consolidated his rule over Saudi territory and established the instruments of central authority. Through his forceful personality, he dominated the rudimentary government that he created in Riyadh. Taking advantage of the Islamic practice of taking four wives, leading members of the House of Saud made alliances through intermarriage with important nomadic and urban families. In consultation with hand-picked advisers, most of them from his immediate family, Abd al-Aziz made all policy decisions, large and small. He divided the kingdom into two viceroyalties, Nejd and Hejaz, and placed his sons, Saud and Faisal, in control of them. In turn, Nejd and Hejaz were subdivided into provinces which were governed by other sons or relatives of Abd al-Aziz. At lower levels, the administration of the viceroyalties was given to Arabs from other countries or to non-native Muslims.

Until the end of the Second World War, the central government had only two ministries: Foreign Affairs, given to Faisal, and Finance, which was under the direction of Abdullah ibn Sulayman. The kingdom had no political parties and no formal governmental procedure. The Qur'an was the constitution, and

Pilgrims prostrate themselves around the Ka'aba, an ancient shrine that Muslims consider the holiest place in the world. By taking control of the Islamic holy cities Mecca and Medina, Abd al-Aziz and his descendants assumed responsibility for ensuring that Muslims could safely make the *hajj*.

Sharia, a body of rules proscribing the behavior of Muslims in all areas of life, was the law. The administration of justice was placed in the hands of the modern descendants of Muhammad ibn Abd al-Wahhab, the Al Sheikh family.

Abd al-Aziz was aware that Saudi possession of the holy cities of Mecca and Medina brought responsibilities. In the summer of 1926 he convened an Islamic Congress at Mecca in order to assure Muslims around the world that the House of Saud would be a responsible guardian of the two Holy Mosques. Muslims from around the world had become nervous when in 1924 Wahhabi clerics had orchestrated the destruction of the tombs of the Shia Imams, including the tomb of Fatima, the Prophet's daughter. Abd al-Aziz put the fears of the world's Muslims to rest. Consequently, pilgrims flocked to Mecca during each of the *hajj* seasons. To this day, the protection of the mosques is a primary source of legitimacy for the Saudi ruling house; in 1986 Saudi King Fahd adopted the title "Custodian of the Two Holy Places."

Although Abd al-Aziz succeeded in creating a functioning state, there remained the problem of integrating its diverse population. In 1929 Abd al-Aziz was challenged by the Bedouin Ikhwan, who resented the King's readiness to accept aspects of modern urban life. For example, many Ikhwan opposed the King's use of the telephone and telegraph, regarding these as non-Islamic innovations. In addition, they did not like the fact that Abd al-Aziz placed restraints on their raiding activities. In 1929–30 the Ikhwan revolted and were defeated by Abd al-Aziz's forces. Thereafter the Saudi state controlled the nomadic tribes by appointing tribal members to positions of power and (after the 1940s) by allocating to them portions of the kingdom's oil revenues.

At the same time, Abd al-Aziz faced other challenges in the Hejaz. The Hejazis were more liberal in their attitudes than the Nejdi Wahhabis, and generally resented the incorporation of their region into the Saudi state. Abd al-Aziz dealt with Hejazi discontent by bringing key figures into the government and by providing Hejazi merchant families opportunities to take advantage of the trade outlets in the kingdom opened by market unification.

Abd al-Aziz adopted a more heavyhanded approach toward the Shiites of al-Hasa, who also felt alienated by the success of the Saudi-Wahhabi movement. In order to diminish Shia identity, Abd al-Aziz encouraged Wahhabi Muslims to settle in al-Hasa and limited public observance of Shia religious practices and devotion. Not until massive protests by the Shia in the 1980s and 1990s did the House of Saud relax its restrictions on the kingdom's Shia population.

The Discovery of Oil

Saudi Arabia's economic prospects were initially bleak. In fact, in 1932 it was one of the poorest countries in the world. However, in 1938 Standard Oil of California discovered oil, an event that utterly transformed the kingdom.

In 1933 Abd al-Aziz had granted Standard Oil of California (later reorganized as the Arabian American Oil Company, or ARAMCO) a concession to extract and transport whatever oil might be found in Saudi Arabia. The company had reason to suspect that significant quantities of petroleum were available in the eastern province of Dhahran. The previous year it had found oil in Bahrain. Abd al-Aziz received the news of the first strike, at an oil well called Dammam no. 7, with unconcealed joy, despite the fact that the terms of the concession favored Standard Oil at the expense of the Saudis.

The outbreak of World War II in 1939 severely hampered the production of Saudi oil. Only after the war, in the late 1940s and early 1950s, did circumstances allow the full and proper exploitation of Saudi Arabia's oil

(Right) Traces of oil blow from the top of Dammam number 7 well, the first major oil strike in Saudi Arabia, circa 1938. (Below) Representatives of the House of Saud and Standard Oil of California sign an agreement giving the American company the right to search for oil in Saudi Arabia, 1933.

resources. In the 1950s, the Saudis renegotiated the original concession to allow the kingdom 50 percent of the profits earned by ARAMCO. Saudis tended to regard the kingdom's new oil wealth as a divine blessing on the land that had given birth to Islam.

During most of World War II Saudi Arabia remained officially neutral. Nevertheless, Abd al-Aziz tacitly favored the Allies and allowed the

King Abd al-Aziz ibn Saud meets U.S. President Franklin D. Roosevelt on board the U.S.S. *Quincy*, 1945. At their meeting the king guaranteed access to Saudi oil in exchange for the promise of U.S. protection.

Americans to build an airfield at Dhahran. On February 14, 1945, just as the war was drawing to a close, Abd al-Aziz met with U.S. President Franklin Roosevelt on board a U.S. warship at the Great Bitter Lake on the Suez Canal. During the meeting, the two leaders talked about the shape of the post-war world. Abd al-Aziz expressed Arab concerns about Jewish immigration to Palestine, which he believed should cease. Despite FDR's non-committal response to this concern, the two leaders did come to a basic understanding. In return for an American pledge to guarantee the independence of Saudi Arabia, Abd al-Aziz promised the United States a steady supply of Saudi oil. In March 1945 Abd al-Aziz declared war on the Axis Powers, a decision that eased the kingdom's entry into the United Nations after the war.

In 1944, Abd al-Aziz joined with the governments of Egypt, Iraq, Lebanon, Syria, Transjordan, and a representative of the Arabs of Palestine in signing an agreement to form the League of Arab States. Henceforth, Abd al-Aziz put himself forward as a champion of Arab independence. The fact that Saudi Arabia was one of the few Islamic countries of Africa and Asia not to have been colonized by Western countries added to his prestige as an influential Arab leader. Abd al-Aziz also gained credit in the Arab world for his strong opposition to the state of Israel, which he believed had been created at the expense of the Arabs of Palestine. With other Arab states, he refused to recognize the legitimacy of the Jewish state after it declared independence in May 1948.

By the early 1950s, however, Abd al-Aziz was a shadow of his former self. Beset with infirmities and confined to a wheelchair, he withdrew from public life. However, before he died in 1953, he designated his son Saud to succeed him.

Wealth from the exploitation of oil transformed the poor states on the Arabian Peninsula, fueling a construction boom. (Opposite) A modern bank building constructed in Kuwait during the mid-1960s. (Right) A riot in Aden, 1967. Conflict in Yemen forced the Saudis to spend more on defending the kingdom.

3 Political Developments in the Gulf

The tribal chieftains of the smaller Gulf States had come under British protection in the 19th century. However, by the 1960s British influence in the Gulf region had significantly diminished, paving the way for the political independence of these states.

In the first four decades of the 20th century, Kuwait was an impoverished country. Its income was badly affected by the Great Depression, and by the introduction on the world market of cultured pearls, mostly from Japan, which undercut the region's pearling industry. However, as was the case in Saudi Arabia, the discovery of oil transformed the country's economy and politics. In 1934 Kuwait's ruler, Ahmad al-Jabir al-Sabah, signed a concession that granted Gulf Oil and British Petroleum the right to prospect for oil in the sheikhdom. Oil exports began in 1946. Over the following decades the ruling Al Sabah family used the revenues to construct roads, port facilities, schools, and hospitals, and to establish a comprehensive welfare system for Kuwaiti nationals. Because of the oil money that it received, the ruling family found that it no longer had to depend on the financial support of the country's merchant families. As a result, the ruling family increased its power by reducing the role of the merchants in government. The merchants agreed to the new situation in return for the financial security provided them by the country's oil wealth.

Britain Withdraws from the Gulf

In 1961 Great Britain, which had long held control over Kuwait's foreign affairs, granted the emirate full independence. Two years later the Emir Abdullah convened an elected consultative body—the national assembly—the first of its kind in the Gulf. Although the assembly had little real power, it marked Kuwait as one of the most politically dynamic states in the Arab Gulf region. In common with Saudi Arabia and other Gulf states, Kuwait became dependent on foreign labor and professional expertise as it built up a modern infrastructure and economy. By 1964, foreign residents outnumbered Kuwaiti nationals.

In 1968 Britain announced its intention to withdraw its forces from all bases east of Suez within three years. For the old treaty states of the Gulf, the prospect of life without British protection was alarming. The rulers of the

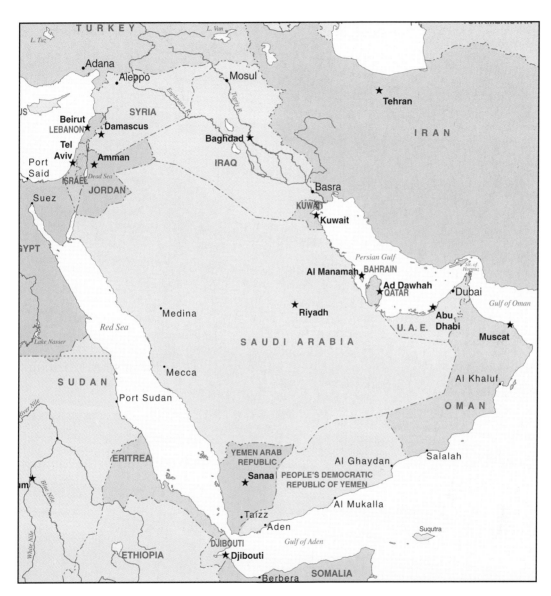

Map of the Arabian Peninsula, 1975. North and South Yemen merged in 1990.

emirates were worried that Saudi Arabia and Iran would take advantage of the power vacuum to dominate them. There were legitimate reasons for concern—Iran had long claimed Bahrain, a majority Shia state, and in the early 20th century the Saudis had made several efforts to extend their influence over various Gulf emirates. In order to prevent takeover by one or other of these countries, the rulers of the small Gulf emirates discussed the possibility of joining together in a unitary state.

In 1971 the rulers of seven former trucial states agreed to form the United Arab Emirates (U.A.E.). However, the people of Bahrain chose through a United Nations referendum to remain independent under the Al Khalifa ruling family. Qatar likewise chose to go its own way. Three of the seven emirates that comprised the U.A.E.—Abu Dhabi, Dubai, and Sharja—possessed considerable oil wealth. During the 1970s they used their oil revenues to transform their city-states into gleaming metropolises. By the 1980s, approximately 80 percent of the population of the United Arab Emirates was made up of foreign workers and managers.

Unlike the smaller Arab Gulf states, Oman had managed to remain independent of British control, although it was heavily dependent on British financial and military assistance. Under Sultan ibn Taimur, who ruled from 1932 to 1970, Oman became an isolated backwater. Little development took place during the reign of this very conservative monarch, even after Oman's relatively modest oil exports began to bring in revenue in the 1960s. During this period, the British helped the Sultan establish his authority in the country's rugged, tribal interior, and helped him defeat Marxist-oriented separatist rebels in Oman's Dhofar province.

In 1970 Sultan ibn Taimur was overthrown by his England-educated son, Qaboos, who began the process of modernizing the country. Under Qaboos roads, schools and hospitals were built. Much of the development was aimed at Dhofar in an attempt to address the simmering discontent toward the central government that remained there.

Political Developments in Saudi Arabia

In Saudi Arabia, King Saud's reign (1953–1964) overlapped with the emergence of Egyptian President Gamal Abdel Nasser. Nasser challenged the Islamic monarchies of Arabia through his appeal to secular Pan-Arabism and socialism. He believed that the traditional and conservative rulers of Arabia were reactionaries who prevented the Arabs from progressing. King Saud

Qaboos ibn Said gained power in Oman by overthrowing his father, Said ibn Taimur, in a bloodless coup in July 1970. Since taking power Qaboos has used revenue from oil to build his country's infrastructure and has invested in an educational system that is among the finest in the Arab world.

Members of the Saudi-funded Muslim World League speak with a visitor at an exhibition in Vancouver. The League was instrumental in spreading the tenets of Wahhabi Islam beyond Saudi Arabia.

chose to confront Nasser's challenge, financing a plot to assassinate the Egyptian president. The plot, which failed, had the effect of isolating Saudi

Arabia in the Arab world and of making the Saudi royal house the special target of Nasser's verbal attacks. Soon other secular revolutionary Arab regimes, such as those in Syria and Iraq, were castigating the House of Saud.

As part of its effort to gain allies against Nasser and the Arab nationalists, Saudi Arabia established close ties with Egypt's Muslim Brotherhood, one of the Arab world's most influential Islamic fundamentalist movements. In order to avoid persecution at the hands of Nasser, many members of the Muslim Brotherhood fled to Saudi Arabia. The Saudi regime welcomed these refugees, many of whom were well-trained professionals. They were employed in the kingdom as preachers and administrators, and influenced many young Saudis to adopt aspects of the Muslim Brotherhood's ideology. Among the Egyptians who relocated to Saudi Arabia was Muhammad Qutb, younger brother of the influential Islamic fundamentalist thinker Sayyid Qutb. Muhammad Qutb found a job teaching at Mecca's Umm al-Qura University.

As an additional counterweight to Nasserism, the Saudi monarchy founded the Muslim World League in 1962. The league opened offices in countries around the world to propagate the tenets of Wahhabi Islam and distribute copies of the Qur'an free of charge. For the first time in history, identical Islamic books could be found from one end of the Muslim world to the other. The Muslim World League not only worked to dampen the appeal of Arab nationalism, it began the process by which Saudi Arabian Wahhabism was popularized globally.

However, ibn Saud's lack of attention to the state's finances drove the kingdom to the brink of bankruptcy. The kingdom's fiscal problems were so serious that the International Monetary Fund urged ibn Saud to ban all imports with the exception of food, medicine, and textiles. In 1964 a coalition of Saudi family members agreed that power should be transferred to Crown Prince Faisal, and ibn Saud was forced to step aside.

Faisal's reign (1964–75) was characterized by rapid growth and development. He used Saudi Arabia's growing oil wealth to build a modern infrastructure of roads and port facilities and to establish a welfare program that provided Saudi citizens with health care and education. Against the wishes of the conservative religious establishment, he was instrumental in introducing television to the kingdom. Faisal regulated development through the Central Planning Organization, which set an ambitious agenda of five-year plans. In order to effectively manage the economic development of the country, the king broadened the role of government.

Faisal also began a program of educational expansion. During his reign new university campuses, both religious and secular, were constructed and thousands of young Saudis were sent abroad to study, mainly at American universities. Faisal made sure that the new ministries and service agencies were staffed by graduates from the local and foreign universities.

Conflict in Southern Arabia

The most significant foreign policy issue affecting the Saudi regime in the 1960s involved developments in the neighboring country of Yemen. In 1962, factions within Yemen's armed forces carried out a coup against the monarch, Imam Muhammad al-Badr. Inspired and supported by Nasser, the coup leaders abolished the monarchy and proclaimed the existence of the Yemen Arab Republic. The revolution was supported by intellectuals, workers, and students—the same social groups that supported revolutionary politics elsewhere in the Arab world. However, the rebels failed to subdue the royalist forces. When Imam al-Badr began rallying tribes in support of his return to the throne, Yemen was plunged into civil war. Each party turned to outside powers for support, thereby transforming the war into a regional conflict. The revolutionary republican regime of Abdullah al-Sallal received military assistance from Nasser, while the royalists in the north were aided by the Saudi government. By 1966, Egyptian forces in Yemen numbered nearly 70,000. King Faisal did not commit Saudi troops to the struggle, but he did pour money and weapons into the royalist cause and allowed royalist forces to infiltrate Yemen from Saudi territory.

King Faisal (right) walks with Egyptian president Gamal Abdel Nasser on the way to an Arab League meeting in Cairo, 1970. Throughout the 1960s the Egyptian and Saudi regimes found themselves competing for influence in the Arab world.

By the late 1960s Yemenis on each side decided to enter into negotiations. Egypt, smarting from its massive defeat by Israel in the June 1967 Arab-Israeli War, acceded to the demands of both sides to withdraw its forces from Yemen. Accordingly, the Yemenis agreed upon the Compromise of 1970, which established a republican government that made room for members of the royalist cause. The royalists agreed that the imam and his family were not to play any role whatsoever in the new state, and the imam went into exile in Britain.

A New Threat

Although the negotiated settlement ended the immediate Egyptian threat to the Saudi regime, developments in south Arabia continued to threaten the security of the Saudi monarchy. In 1967 Britain withdrew from the Aden Protectorate. Immediately, the void was filled by the locally organized National Liberation Front, which established the Marxist People's Democratic Republic of South Yemen. As a radical revolutionary state, South Yemen followed Nasser's lead in supporting the overthrow of all traditional monarchies in the Arabian Peninsula. King Faisal responded to the new threat by attempting to foment discord between the newly created Yemen Arab Republic in the north and the People's Democratic Republic of the south. Throughout the 1980s the two Yemens viewed one another, and Saudi Arabia, with suspicion.

The radicalization of the Yemens and the rise of popular liberation movements elsewhere in the peninsula, such as Dhofar in Oman, prompted King Faisal to improve Saudi Arabia's armed forces. The confrontation in north Yemen revealed that the Saudi military was not strong enough to check Egypt's forces. Indeed, it became clear that the Saudi armed forces might not be able to put down an internal uprising. The king increased the defense budget to over $2 billion dollars in 1970 and over the decade the Saudis allocated between 35 and 40 percent of their total annual revenues to defense and security costs. The government purchased the most sophisticated military technology available. A special effort was made to build up the air force. The Saudis purchased most of the weaponry from the United States, which signed a number of weapons contracts with the Saudis in the 1970s and 1980s.

With the formation of OPEC, the oil-rich Arab states had a lever with which to affect international politics. (Opposite) Oil ministers from OPEC member nations attend a meeting in Vienna. (Right) The Arab oil embargo of 1973–74 led to long lines at gas stations in the United States.

4 The Politics of Oil

Saudi Arabia's development projects and military spending were funded by growing oil revenues. In order to have greater influence over the price of oil, in 1960 Saudi Arabia joined four other countries—Iran, Iraq, Kuwait, and Venezuela—to establish the Organization of Petroleum Exporting Countries (OPEC). Soon after, Abu Dhabi, Algeria, Ecuador, Gabon, Indonesia, Libya, Nigeria, and Qatar joined. A parallel group, the Organization of Arab Petroleum Exporting Countries (OAPEC), made up entirely of Arab oil-producing countries, was founded in 1968. The purpose of the two organizations, especially for member states from the Middle East, was to influence and control the oil industries. Earlier in the century, European and American oil companies had taken advantage of the Arab rulers' lack of knowledge about the industry to gain concessions that benefited the companies but not the host nations. By banding together, the producing countries aimed to use their collective bargaining power to pressure Western companies to increase oil prices.

OPEC's first success came in 1969, when Libya sought an increase in its royalty fees. When the oil companies refused Libya's demands, it decreased its production, causing a panic among European nations, which received 20 percent of their oil needs from the North African country. Unable to secure alternative sources, the oil companies relented. Under the leadership of Saudi Arabia's Sheikh Yamani, OPEC's chief negotiator, the Gulf countries also won the right to determine the base price of their oil.

The OPEC member states were able to gain leverage over the oil companies because of the increased global demand for oil in the 1960s and 1970s. With the rise of gasoline-fueled cars and oil-powered industries, the economically developed countries of the West and Asia came more and more to depend on petroleum from the Middle East. As a result, Saudi Arabia alone was supplying 13 percent of the world's oil by 1973.

Building upon their early success, the OPEC countries of the Middle East came to demand ownership of the oil companies themselves. In 1973 Saudi Arabia acquired a 25 percent interest in ARAMCO, and by 1980 the kingdom had purchased 100 percent of the company's assets. The Saudis changed the name to the Saudi Arabian Oil Company (Saudi ARAMCO). At the same time, the Saudis gained controlling interests in supplementary activities such as refining and marketing.

The Power of Oil

Saudi Arabia's power as an oil producer was shown after the 1973 war between Israel and its Arab neighbors. The war is often referred to in the West and Israel as the Yom Kippur War, the Jewish holy day on which it began. The conflict began on October 6 when Egypt attacked Israeli forces in the Sinai Peninsula, while Syrian forces attacked Israeli positions in the Golan Heights. (Israel had captured both of these areas in the June 1967 "Six Day" War, and had occupied them since that time.) Taken by surprise, the Israelis were pushed back in Sinai. However, the Israeli forces managed to regroup and launch a counteroffensive with the assistance of the United States, which airlifted weapons to Israel and provided $2.2 billion in aid.

King Faisal was disturbed by the support of the United States and its western allies for the State of Israel. In a move intended to punish these countries, Saudi Arabia and 10 other Arab oil producers cut back the amount of oil they produced. Other non-Arab members of OPEC did the same. In addition, Saudi Arabia, Libya, and other Arab states imposed an oil embargo on the United States and the Netherlands; the Arabs targeted the Netherlands because it was the chief entry point for Saudi oil into Europe.

Following the conclusion of the war at the end of October, U.S. Secretary of State Henry Kissinger visited Cairo, Damascus, and Jerusalem in an effort to forge a lasting peace between the Arab states and Israel. As a result of this effort, Saudi-American relations improved and in March 1974 Saudi Arabia and the other Arab states (except Libya) lifted the embargo. However, oil prices remained at an all-time high. Where a barrel of oil had traded for $2.74

in early 1973, by 1974 the price had increased to $11.65 per barrel. Saudi Arabia took advantage of the price hike by increasing production, and billions of petrodollars flowed into the kingdom. King Faisal used this additional revenue to fund the most ambitious Saudi development program to date. Between the mid-1970s and mid 1980s, roads, airports, office buildings, and port facilities were built. Oil money also facilitated the construction of new universities, such as Umm al-Qura University in Mecca and King Faisal University in Dammam and Hofuf.

The new oil wealth enabled Saudi Arabia to influence the policies of other Arab and Muslim countries. By providing financial support to countries and organizations that were on the "front line" against Israel, such as the Palestine Liberation Organization, Egypt, and Syria, Saudi Arabia won the good will of regimes in the region, including several that had previously been opposed to the conservative Saudi monarchy. Greater oil revenues also enabled the Muslim World League to export the Wahhabi interpretation of Islam by building *madrassas* (Islamic schools) throughout the Islamic world.

Changes in the Kingdom

King Faisal did not live to see the fruits of the massive development projects he had initiated. In March 1975, during Faisal's weekly *majlis*, or public audience, he was assassinated. Faisal was succeeded by his half-brother, Crown Prince Khalid, who ruled from 1975 to 1982. King Khalid loved falconry and camping in the desert with the Bedouins, and was a more traditional figure than Faisal. Often in ill health, he delegated many of his responsibilities to his half-brother, Crown Prince Fahd. Fahd was a capable administrator who kept the modernization process on track, despite a slump in revenues that occurred after 1981 as new sources of crude were discovered and the global price of oil dropped.

Two major social changes took place during the boom years of the 1970s and 1980s. One was the entry into the kingdom of hundreds of thousands of foreign workers. As in other Gulf countries, Saudi Arabia was beset with a shortage of manpower, and there was an acute need for laborers and professionals from abroad. By 1980 there were approximately 2.5 million foreigners living and working in Saudi Arabia, representing 52 percent of the workforce. The largest groups came from other Arab countries, including Egypt, the occupied Palestinian territories, Jordan, and neighboring North Yemen. Other workers came from Pakistan, India, South Korea, and the Philippines. About 100,000 North Americans and Europeans came to the kingdom, attracted by lucrative employment opportunities. Expatriates who worked in the kingdom on a long-term basis became part of Saudi society, although very few were granted Saudi citizenship. Nevertheless, the Saudis were worried that the immigrants might introduce values antithetical to Wahhabi Islam, and so isolated them from the native society. Westerners, for example, were largely limited to the large Saudi ARAMCO compound near Dhahran.

The other major change was the transformation of Saudi society. As a result of the modernization programs of Abd al-Aziz ibn Saud and King Faisal, a new middle class emerged made up of businessmen, doctors, teachers, and higher paid workers. However, rather than incorporate the modernizing middle class into the state's decision-making processes, the House of Saud continued to govern autocratically, refusing to allow political parties, trade unions, and other representative groups to form. To a large degree, the state's ban on representative bodies was made acceptable to the educated classes by the large and reasonably efficient welfare programs that served them and other Saudi citizens. It would not be until 1992 that the king would appoint a formal Majlis al-Shura (consultative council) to advise him in matters of state.

The Religious Establishment

During the second half of the 20th century, the *ulama*—including the Al Sheikh family—continued to wield considerable moral authority over Saudi

Men work on a Saudi ARAMCO offshore oil platform, 1970s. As they built modern infrastructure and economies, Saudi Arabia and the other Gulf states became dependent on foreign labor.

Arabian society. From the 1920s onward, this clerical authority included public morality committees organized to ensure acceptable standards of behavior among the people. The committees enforced strict female segregation and prohibited smoking, drinking, and dancing.

Although religious scholars enjoyed considerable authority in regulating public and private life at the local level, they were subordinate to the Grand Mufti, the highest legal authority in the country, who stood as the final arbiter of what was permitted and what was forbidden in the kingdom. All the official *ulama*, including the Grand Mufti, drew their pay from government departments where they were employed or from the religious universities where they taught.

In return for patronage and support from the state, the House of Saud expected the *ulama* to ratify and provide legitimacy to the regime's policies. The clerics' legitimizing function was most notable when used to justify state actions that ran counter to popular feelings and religious sensitivities. Like Saudi Arabia's middle class, the clerical establishment was willing to support the ruling house in return for guarantees concerning the *ulama's* secure position in the state and society.

The 1960s and 1970s was a period of tremendous economic growth for Saudi Arabia. Using oil wealth to its advantage, the Saudis became major players in the politics of the Middle East. Yet not all was well in the kingdom. Developments that took place in the 1970s set the stage for a number of challenges that would rock the Saudi regime in the 1980s and 1990s.

Events in 1979 threatened to destabilize the Arab monarchies. (Opposite) A communist banner flies over the presidential palace in Kabul, Afghanistan, which was invaded and occupied by the Soviet Union. (Right) After gaining power in Iran, Ayatollah Khomeini attempted to export his Shiite Islamic Revolution to the neighboring Gulf states.

5 Domestic and Regional Challenges

In the history of the Middle East 1979 was a momentous year. That year Islamic revolution broke out in Iran, a country where most of the residents were Shia Muslims, in response to the flawed policies of the Shah, Mohammed Reza Pahlavi. Although Iran possessed considerable oil wealth, the revenues were spread unevenly among the population. As a result, during the 1960s and 1970s the gap between the rich, represented by the aristocratic and big business classes, and the poor, increased. In addition, the Shah imposed Western, secular culture on Iran's people, many of whom were traditional and religiously conservative. Under the leadership of the Ayatollah Ruhollah Khomeini (1900–1989), the Iranian people overthrew the Shah and established an Islamic republic with Khomeini as their leader.

That year, too, the Soviet Union invaded Afghanistan, setting the stage for a decade-long *jihad* by Afghans and Muslim volunteer fighters from around the world. (One of these fighters, a Saudi national named Osama bin Laden, would later attain notoriety as leader of the terrorist organization al-Qaeda.)

Also in 1979 a group of religious rebels seeking to overthrow the Saudi dynasty seized the Grand Mosque in Mecca. The takeover was a landmark event in the history of the kingdom. The group's commander was Juhaiman al-Utaibi. The group's spiritual leader, Muhammad ibn Abdullah al-Qahtani, called himself the Mahdi (the "guided one"). This is the name of a messianic figure whose appearance, many Muslims believe, will usher in the Last Days. Most of Juhaiman's and al-Qahtani's followers came from tribes that had spearheaded the Ikhwan revolts against Abd al-Aziz ibn Saud 50 years earlier, although support for the movement also came from students, the urban lower classes, and from foreign laborers.

On November 20, the last day of the ritual *hajj* pilgrimage, the rebels, numbering between 400 and 500, struck. They used the mosque's public address system to broadcast their demands, calling for a return to the society of the first centuries of Islam, which the royal family, they said, had corrupted. They demanded the elimination of Western influences in the kingdom, including such things as photography, and the severing of economic and political ties with Western nations. In addition, the rebels blamed the *ulama* for failing to condemn policies that betrayed Islam.

The House of Saud understood that it had to take decisive action. Its legitimacy hinged on its ability to protect the holy places. On November 24 King Khalid received from Grand Mufti ibn Baz an Islamic legal opinion (*fatwa*) authorizing the use of force against the insurgents. The *fatwa* was necessary because in normal circumstances the spilling of blood was not allowed on the holy ground of the Meccan sanctuary. For two weeks the Saudi armed forces, aided by French commandos, battled the rebels. In the course of the fighting al-Qahtani was killed. After the surviving rebels surrendered, Juhaiman al-Utaibi and 62 others were publicly beheaded in accordance with Sharia law.

Juhaiman's and al-Qahtani's challenge to the Saudi dynasty had received little overt support from the general population. Nevertheless, the revolt caused the Saudi ruling elite to consider that similar, religiously focused anti-regime uprisings could take place in the future. The Saudis were correct in this assessment. The uprising was the beginning of a more wide-reaching Islamist opposition movement that would command attention in the 1990s. In order to protect the regime from similar outbreaks, the ruling family strengthened the security services with the assistance of advisers from the U.S. Central Intelligence Agency (CIA).

Other measures were taken as well. It had become clear to the Saudi rulers that the main source of the rebels' rage was the gap between the professed piety of the regime and its apparent willingness to make compromises with secular modernity, which led them to charge the regime with hypocrisy. It was also evident that oil wealth had, as the rebels had claimed, corrupted the morals of many Saudi princes. In order to placate dissent and shore up its legitimacy, the ruling house increased its support of the *ulama*, some of whom shared the basic grievance of the rebels that the kingdom was drifting away from its founding ideals. Authorities allowed the *ulama* to implement even stricter regulations on public morality, with an emphasis on women's role in society. For example, an earlier measure that allowed female television announcers was reversed. The state also poured billions of dollars into the construction of mosques, religious schools, and missionary endeavors. However, by supporting the strict application of Wahhabism, the House of Saud helped to create a religious revival throughout Saudi society that would come back to haunt the regime.

The Challenge from Iran

No sooner had the insurrection of Juhaiman al-Utaibi been crushed than a Shia uprising occurred in Saudi Arabia's eastern Hasa Province, location of the kingdom's principal oil fields. The unrest coincided with the observance of Ashura, the tenth day of the Islamic month of Muharram, on which the Shiite Imam Hussein was martyred in 680 C.E. The protesters focused on specific grievances: the right to observe Shiite religious rituals; an end to discrimination; a greater share in the state's oil revenues; more job and educational opportunities; and repair of the crumbling infrastructure in Shiite towns and cities. In addition, the protesters condemned the House of Saud's close alliance with the United States.

The symbolism of Imam Hussein's struggle against injustice fanned the flames of protest, as did the success of the Shia-oriented Islamic Revolution across the Gulf in Iran. Khomeini's new Iranian regime beamed radio broadcasts into Saudi Arabia attacking the monarchy. Shiite protesters in Saudi

Arabia set fire to industrial plants and banks and were fired upon by the National Guard. The unrest lasted well into 1980. The Saudis responded to the Shia uprising by initiating development projects in economically neglected Hasa, including construction of schools and hospitals and an electrical network. In the long term, the strategy of dampening popular disaffection in Hasa through public works programs paid dividends. In the years that followed, the province was quiet as the two religious communities of Saudi Arabia—Wahhabi and Shia—worked towards conciliation.

Yet Iran remained a threat. Like other revolutionary movements in history, Khomeini's followers wanted to overthrow the existing order in the Middle East and replace it with something completely new—a network of Islamic states that looked to his leadership. Khomeini regarded the House of Saud and the rulers of other Arab Gulf states with contempt. In his view, they were American lackeys, unpopular and corrupt dictatorships that suppressed their Shiite populations. In addition to encouraging the Shia of Eastern Saudi Arabia

Once he became ruler of Saudi Arabia in 1982, King Fahd took steps to prevent Khomeini's influence from spreading. His government provided aid to Iraq, which had started a war against Iran in 1980, and increased funding to conservative Wahhabi religious leaders to counter those who felt the Saudi regime was too secular.

to rebel, he supported the Shia population of Bahrain in its efforts to gain rights against the domination of the Sunni Al Khalifa ruling family. Throughout the 1980s Khomeini attempted to assert his influence by sending ideologically motivated Iranian pilgrims on the *hajj*. In July 1987 clashes between Iranian pilgrims and Saudi police left 402 dead.

In 1982 King Khalid died and was succeeded by his half-brother Fahd ibn Abd al-Aziz. Fahd's half-brother, Abdullah, commander of the National Guard, was named crown prince. Under King Fahd the Saudis responded to the challenge posed by Iran. Just as the House of Saud had confronted Nasserism in Yemen and elsewhere in the 1960s, so now it pledged to halt and perhaps even to roll back the Iranian-sponsored Shia revival. To this end, the Saudis wrested from the United States a solid guarantee that America would help protect the kingdom from its enemies. The Saudis were dismayed that the Americans had stood by as their ally, the Shah of Iran, fell to Khomeini's supporters. U.S. President Jimmy Carter had addressed this Saudi concern in his January 1980 State of the Union Address with a pledge that any Iranian or Soviet aggression in the Gulf would be considered as an attack on the United States. During the presidency of Ronald Reagan (1981–1989), the Saudis continued their practice of purchasing weapons from the United States, although they also looked to other countries for arms, including Great Britain and China.

The Saudis cultivated close bonds with Sunni leaders and groups that were similarly interested in containing the Iranian Revolution, including President Zia al-Haqq of Pakistan. Throughout the 1980s the Saudi regime helped to fund Sunni *madrassas* in Pakistan, which taught the Wahhabi interpretation of Islam. Through the offices of the Saudi-sponsored Muslim World League, the regime subsidized Sunni causes through charities and sent Wahhabi preachers around the world. In undertaking these endeavors, Saudi Arabia presented itself as the global champion of conservative Sunni Islam.

War in the Gulf

During the Iran-Iraq War (1980–88), Saudi Arabia threw its weight behind Iraqi dictator Saddam Hussein. Iraq had invaded Iran in September 1980 to prevent the Iranian Revolution from spreading into Iraq. Saddam suspected that many Iraqi Shiites, who made up some 60 percent of the country's total population, were attracted to Khomeini's cause and feared that they might attempt to break away from Iraq. An additional motive for Iraq's invasion was to gain control of the Shatt al-Arab waterway, which since 1975 had been divided between Iraq and Iran. The waterway was Iraq's only access to the Persian Gulf, and Hussein wanted it all.

Saddam Hussein expected a quick victory over Iran. The Khomeini regime had yet to fully consolidate its power and Iran's army was in disarray. However, the Iraqi invasion had the effect of rallying the Iranian population around Khomeini's party in order to repel the Iraqi enemy. Following initial Iraqi successes, the war quickly turned into a stalemate. Although the House of Saud and other Arab Gulf countries had no love for the secular regime of Saddam Hussein, they supported his war effort against Iran in the hope that Hussein might crush the Islamic Revolution and spare the region further Iranian encroachment. The United States also tilted toward Saddam Hussein in order to maintain the region's stability.

In an effort to create a regional front against Iran, Saudi Arabia met in May 1981 in Abu Dhabi with representatives from the United Arab Emirates, Kuwait, Bahrain, Qatar, and Oman to form the Gulf Cooperation Council (GCC). According to the organization's charter, its members were to promote regional security and protect one another's sovereignty against outside aggression. In addition, the charter promoted free trade agreements and the funding of development projects among member states. Over the course of the Iran-Iraq War, Saudi Arabia and other GCC members provided Saddam Hussein with billions of dollars in loans and outright gifts to finance his war effort.

In order to undermine the GCC's support for Iraq, Iran began to attack GCC oil tankers, which carried much of Iraq's oil. Most of these attacks were

Soon after the Iran-Iraq War broke out in September 1980, Saudi Arabia and the Arab Gulf states formed the Gulf Cooperation Council, an agreement for mutual defense as well as economic cooperation.

aimed at Kuwaiti vessels. Eager to keep the sea lanes open, the United States in 1987 allowed GCC ships to fly the U.S. flag. Any Iranian attack on these reflagged ships would be considered an attack on the United States, and U.S. naval vessels were sent to the Persian Gulf to protect the tankers. This threat of U.S. retaliation would allow the oil tankers to dock at Iraq's ports, thus guaranteeing the country revenue that would allow it to continue waging the war. Despite a number of incidents involving the United States and Iran, the strategy was successful.

Saudi Arabia and the Jihad in Afghanistan

Over this period Saudi Arabia also supported the anti-Soviet *jihad* in Afghanistan. Keen to prevent the spread of communism in South Asia and strengthen Sunni Islam against revolutionary Shiism, the Saudis worked with Pakistan's Inter-Services Intelligence Directorate (ISI) in training and funding the Afghan *mujahideen*, or "holy warriors." The monarchy's support of the *jihad* further increased its legitimacy as the defender of the faith in the face of the cultural and political assault on the kingdom.

The conflict in Afghanistan attracted foreign volunteers, many of whom belonged to established Islamist opposition groups from all over the Middle East and Asia. Overwhelmingly, they were Arabs from Egypt, Algeria, and Saudi Arabia. Blocked in their home countries by police action, these Islamist soldiers of fortune considered Afghanistan an appropriate and inviting location to engage the principle of *jihad*. In so doing, they combined conservative Wahhabi ideas with the radical *jihadi* trend common to Egyptian Islamism. This blending of influences was evident in the writings of the famous

The Afghan resistance fighters known as *mujahideen*, who fought the Soviets from 1979 to 1989, were funded in part by the Saudi government. The U.S. Central Intelligence Agency also provided financial aid to the *mujahideen* in order to check the expansion of Soviet power in the Middle East.

Palestinian advocate of the *jihad*, Abdullah Azzam. He took much of his inspiration from the Islamic fundamentalist thinker Qutb but was also a beneficiary of Saudi patronage.

The Afghan war was the defining experience in the life of Osama bin Laden. A native Saudi who grew up in the devotional environment of Wahhabism, bin Laden was the youngest of some 20 surviving sons of Sheikh Muhammad bin Laden, a wealthy building contractor whose company had exclusive right for the construction and repair of all religious buildings in the kingdom, including the holy sites in Mecca and Medina. When Sheikh Muhammad was killed in a helicopter crash in 1968, bin Laden inherited $80 million of his father's fortune. Bin Laden was one of the first Arabs to join the *jihad*. He saw his role there as facilitator and spent his personal fortune to build roads and tunnels for the *mujahideen* and provide pensions to the families of the fallen. He is reputed to have been involved in at least one major battle. His personal piety and willingness to sacrifice comfort and wealth for the cause of Islam endeared him to his fellows.

In 1988 Osama bin Laden formed an organization called al-Qaeda ("the Base"), which was a registry of all the foreign jihadis who had come to Afghanistan. It was the nucleus of the group that would eventually launch attacks against America on September 11, 2001, although in 1988 bin Laden did not yet consider the United States his primary enemy. His concern at this point was with reform in his homeland of Saudi Arabia. Shortly after the Soviets withdrew from Afghanistan in defeat in 1989, bin Laden returned to Saudi Arabia. There, he founded a welfare organization to take care of the thousands of Saudi veterans of the Afghanistan *jihad*.

If the oil-rich states of the Arabian Peninsula are threatened, the United States has pledged it will intervene to defend them. (Opposite) U.S. Marines disembark in the kingdom as part of Operation Desert Shield, 1990. (Right) A Saudi prince greets U.S. Secretary of Defense Robert M. Gates, 2007.

6 The Gulf War and its Aftermath

On August 2, 1990, 100,000 Iraqi soldiers invaded the Emirate of Kuwait. After capturing control of the tiny country, Saddam Hussein annexed Kuwait, declaring it Iraq's 19th province.

The purpose of Saddam's invasion was to gain control of the emirate's oil revenues, which the dictator needed to rebuild Iraq's economy following the eight-year-long war with Iran. In addition, he wanted possession of Kuwait's deep-water port facilities, as the Shatt al-Arab waterway remained divided between Iraq and Iran. Saddam Hussein justified his takeover of

Kuwait by pointing out that Kuwait and the U.A.E. had been exceeding OPEC oil production quotas, which had the effect of driving down oil prices on the world market at a time when Iraq needed maximum revenues from its own oil. Saddam Hussein also accused Kuwait of pumping oil from inside Iraqi territory, and was angry that Kuwait and other Arab Gulf states were pressing him for the repayment of debts incurred in the recent war. The Iraqi dictator believed that those debts should be forgiven because Iraq had protected the region from Iranian domination. Finally, Saddam Hussein made the case that in Ottoman times Kuwait had formed part of the Province of Basra until it was made a British Protectorate in 1899. Because Basra had been incorporated into Iraq when that state was created in 1920, Saddam claimed, Kuwait properly belonged to Iraq.

Saddam's justifications for the invasion did not carry weight with the world community. Overwhelmingly, nations around the globe viewed the annexation of Kuwait as violating the sovereignty of an independent country. The Americans and the Saudis, in particular, were worried that Saddam Hussein would not stop at conquering Kuwait, but intended also to take over the oil fields of neighboring Saudi Arabia. Working though the United Nations, U.S. President George H.W. Bush put together an international coalition to eject Iraq from Kuwait. Significantly, the coalition included Arab states outside of the Gulf, such as Egypt and Syria, which were interested in maintaining the political order in the region as it had existed prior to the invasion.

Traditionally, the Saudis forbade the presence of foreign soldiers in their country. However, in this case Saudi authorities considered it necessary, and Grand Mufti ibn Baz issued a *fatwa* that allowed the United States and its allies to station hundreds of thousands of their troops in the kingdom, both to protect it from possible Iraqi aggression and to prepare for the assault against Iraqi troops in Kuwait. Many ordinary Saudis were not happy with the decision, considering the establishment of allied military bases on Saudi soil as an affront to Islam.

After providing Iraq with an opportunity to withdraw its troops from Kuwait, the allies commenced an aerial bombardment of Iraqi positions in January 1991, followed by a ground assault the next month. The U.S.-led coalition easily defeated the Iraqi army, but did not press on to Baghdad to depose Saddam Hussein. Instead, the allies decided to contain Iraq in order to prevent the dictator from again threatening the states of the Gulf region. As part of this strategy, the United States maintained over 20,000 of its troops in Saudi Arabia following Iraq's defeat.

Aftermath of the Gulf War

Kuwait was physically damaged during the Iraqi invasion. Iraqi troops looted the country and destroyed most of its oil wells. Many Kuwaitis were upset that the ruling Al Sabah family had fled the war for Saudi Arabia while the bulk of the population suffered through the occupation. In order to satisfy growing anger, the Al Sabah reconvened its national assembly, a parliamentary body headed by a prime minister. Males over the age of 21 who could prove that their families had lived in Kuwait prior to 1920 were eligible to vote for candidates to the assembly. In 2006 the franchise was extended to Kuwaiti women.

The war also prompted political reforms in Saudi Arabia. Bowing to U.S. pressure, in March 1992 King Fahd convened a consultative assembly. The

Burning oil wells cast a black pall over Kuwait, March 1991. As Iraqi troops retreated from Kuwait, they did great damage to the emirate's oil infra-structure. The economic and ecological cost was estimated at $160 billion.

Saudi monarch had promised such an assembly in 1980, but had done nothing to bring it into being. The council was comprised of 60 Saudi men selected by the king who would advise him on domestic and foreign policy issues.

In 1995 King Fahd suffered a stroke and his half-brother, Abdullah, assumed the responsibilities of government. Abdullah continued Fahd's policy of building consensus in the kingdom.

However, these political reforms were not sufficient to halt a growing wave of dissatisfaction. Many Saudis were unhappy that American troops remained in the country and that, during the war, the kingdom had depended on non-Muslim military assistance, despite the billions spent by the Saudi monarch on advanced military equipment. They were dismayed also that war expenditures and development projects had turned Saudi Arabia into a debtor nation. Saudi Arabia's problems, they said, were the consequence of the House of Saud's turning away from Islam.

Nearly all of these critics of the regime came from within a movement called the "Sahwa al-Islamiyya" ("Islamic Awakening"), the religious revivalist movement that gripped Saudi universities and other elite institutions from the late 1960s onwards. The "Awakening" activists combined the conservative Wahhabi outlook on social and cultural issues with political activism in the style of the Muslim Brotherhood.

The concerns of the activists were embodied in two documents addressed to the king: the "Letter of Demands" (1991) and the "Memorandum of Advice" (1992). These documents called for reform, rather than radical change, and were sent through Sheikh Abd al-Aziz bin Baz, the kingdom's Grand Mufti, in the hopes of bringing him and the other state *ulama* aboard. The documents had over 100 signatures of leading Saudi citizens. The Saudi regime came down hard on the dissenters. Several, including sheikhs Safar al-Hawali and Salman al-Awda, were imprisoned. Others, such as Muhammad al-Masari and

Sad al-Faqih, were forced to flee the country. Most of the Saudi exiles ended up in London.

The Rise of Al-Qaeda

One of those who signed the "Letter of Demands" was Osama bin Laden. When Saddam Hussein invaded Kuwait, bin Laden approached King Fahd and tried to dissuade him from inviting U.S. troops to the kingdom. He told King Fahd that he could assemble an army of veterans from the anti-Soviet *jihad* in Afghanistan that would rid Kuwait of the Iraqis and protect Saudi Arabia from possible invasion. When the king declined the offer, bin Laden stepped up his criticism of the regime.

In 1991 he left Saudi Arabia for the African country of Sudan, where he was welcomed by that country's Islamic fundamentalist government. In Sudan bin Laden organized and financed a number of small-scale terrorist operations, many against Western targets. He was implicated in a failed plot to assassinate Egyptian president Hosni Mubarak, who had been a strong supporter of U.S. intervention in the 1991 Gulf War. In 1994 the Saudi Arabian government stripped bin Laden of his Saudi citizenship and his family disowned him. Two years later, under pressure from Saudi Arabia and the United States, the government of Sudan expelled him from the country.

Bin Laden relocated to Afghanistan, which had just come under the control of the Taliban, a conservative Islamic fundamentalist movement. The Taliban allowed bin Laden and his al-Qaeda organization to use Afghanistan as a base of operations. From Afghanistan, Osama bin Laden and his associates planned attacks against Western targets. In August 1998 al-Qaeda operatives detonated bombs at the U.S. embassies in Tanzania and Kenya, killing more than 300 people. In October 2000 a suicide bomber damaged the U.S. destroyer *Cole* while it was anchored in the harbor at Aden, Yemen. But the major attack occurred on

Throughout the 1990s and early 2000s, U.S. military personnel serving on the Arabian Peninsula were subject to attacks by terrorist groups. One of the deadliest of these attacks occurred in 1996, when a radical group calling itself Hezbollah in the Hejaz detonated a truck bomb outside the Khobar Towers apartment complex that killed 19 American servicemen and wounded more than 370 people.

Osama bin Laden, a Saudi national, disapproved when the Saudi government permitted non-Muslim soldiers from the United States to be garrisoned in the kingdom. His al-Qaeda organization planned attacks against Western targets outside of Saudi Arabia.

September 11, 2001, when al-Qaeda terrorists hijacked several airplanes and flew them into the World Trade Center in New York City and the Pentagon outside Washington, D.C. The attacks killed nearly 3,000 people.

By striking at the United States, bin Laden hoped to trigger a massive U.S. response that would, in turn, rally Muslims around the world around to al-Qaeda.

In the Wake of the Attacks

The September 11, 2001, terrorist attacks strained the relationship between Saudi Arabia and the United States. Americans were surprised and angry that 15 of the 19 hijackers were Saudi citizens. The United States also complained that charities controlled by Saudi citizens had helped fund the al-Qaeda terrorists, and that Wahhabi missionaries had been spreading anti-American propaganda around the Muslim world. In response to American criticisms, in 2002 Saudi Arabia set up a commission to oversee the operation of all charities in the kingdom. Further, the Saudis made moves to curtail anti-American and anti-Jewish teachings in Saudi schools and universities. For its part, Saudi Arabia blamed the United States for fanning the flames of Islamist extremism by uncritically supporting Israel.

Over the years following the September 11 attacks, anti-American feeling was strong among both the Saudi public and many in the House of Saud. Sensitive to public opinion, Crown Prince Abdullah limited the United States to a single Saudi airbase during the assault on the Taliban and al-Qaeda in Afghanistan, which commenced in October 2001. The Crown Prince also warned the administration of George W. Bush against invading Iraq, arguing that the removal of Saddam Hussein's regime would lead to regional instability. Deprived of Saudi support, the United States depended on bases in Bahrain and Kuwait during the buildup to its 2003 invasion of Iraq.

In addition, in response to what Arabs viewed as U.S. inaction in the Israel-Palestinian peace negotiations, in 2002 Crown Prince Abdullah issued a plan that called for Israel's withdrawal to its pre-1967 borders in return for peace and recognition of Israel's sovereignty by Arab nations, including Saudi Arabia. However, the plan was not generally accepted by other Arab nations on account of its lack of provision for Palestinian refugees.

Despite the House of Saud's criticism of American policy in the Middle East, it remained a U.S. ally and thus was targeted by homegrown Islamist terrorists. The Saudi face of jihadi militancy emerged most visibly from 2003 to 2004, when a network of hardened militants operating under the name "Al-Qaeda on the Arabian Peninsula" began to target U.S. and other Western personnel and interests. This group is typical of more recent al-Qaeda offshoots;

it has operated more or less autonomously of bin Laden and his lieutenant Dr. Ayman al-Zawahiri while adhering to the basic al-Qaeda ideology. Although Al-Qaeda on the Arabian Peninsula is a component of al-Qaeda's global *jihad*, its specific aim is to halt U.S. influence over the countries of the Arabian Peninsula, chiefly Saudi Arabia. According to the organization's theorists, the "cleansing" of the peninsula of American power would weaken the "corrupt" House of Saud, thus rendering it vulnerable to al-Qaeda. The conquest of Saudi Arabia would be the first step in the reestablishment of the global caliphate. The group's attacks were met by force, to the extent that by late 2005 the organization was effectively defeated. However, manifestations of al-Qaeda militancy in Saudi Arabia continue to linger.

The Arabian Peninsula in the 21st Century

In August 2005 King Fahd was laid to rest in an unmarked desert grave. King Abdullah, his successor, is today faced with a number of challenges as Saudi Arabia enters the new century. One potential problem is Saudi Arabia's rising population, especially the growing number of young people. Will the kingdom be able to absorb the population explosion and provide meaningful jobs for its university graduates? Another challenge facing the ruling house is the rising demand from Saudi Arabia's middle class for a more open political system. Will Saudi Arabia remain an old-style monarchy or will the power of the Saudis be tempered by a constitution that allows others in society to have a meaningful voice? Yet a third issue relates to security. The al-Qaeda ideology continues to attract young Saudis and direct them toward violent confrontation with the regime. The ruling family must find a way to address the causes of this extreme form of dissidence.

Saudi Arabia must also contend with the rising power in the Gulf of the Islamic Republic of Iran. Since the 1970s the Saudi kingdom and Iran have been at loggerheads. Tension between the two countries threatens once more to flare up following the fall of Saddam Hussein at the hands of the United States and its allies. Will Iran establish influence in Iraq's Shia-dominated southern region? What will the effect of Iranian dominance in the region be on Saudi Arabia's Shia population? How will Saudi Arabia react to Iran's challenge?

Finally, will Saudi Arabia's relationship with the United

Saudi Arabia's King Abdullah waves after addressing the kingdom's Majlis al-Shura, or consultative council, which was formed in 1992. Today the monarchs of the Arabian Peninsula are assailed from two directions: secular moderates wish to open up the traditional political systems and allow greater public participation in decision-making, while Islamists seek an even stricter application of Islamic law in everyday life.

States remain strong, despite the pressures exerted on that relationship by the September 11 attacks? One thing is certain: Saudi Arabia, with its oil wealth, educated population, and strategic location, will continue to be an important and influential state in the decades to come.

1744:	Muhammad ibn Abd al-Wahhab settles in Diriyah and allies himself with Emir Muhammad ibn Saud.
1818:	Employing Muhammad Ali of Egypt, the Ottomans destroy the first Saudi state.
1884:	Muhammad Al Rashid, emir of Hail and vassal of the Ottomans, takes over Nejd.
1902:	Abd al-Aziz ibn Saud captures Riyadh from the Rashidis and confronts the Ottomans.
1916:	In June Sharif Husayn ibn Ali, Hashemite emir of Mecca, begins the Arab Revolt and declares Hejaz independent and himself King of Arabia.
1921:	Aziz ibn Saud proclaims himself "Sultan of Nejd."
1925:	Jedda surrenders to the Saudis. Abd al-Aziz ibn Saud is proclaimed "King of Hejaz."
1929:	Abd al-Aziz ibn Saud crushes the Ikhwan revolt.
1932:	Abd-al-Aziz ibn Saud joins Nejd with Hejaz to form the Kingdom of Saudi Arabia.
1933:	Standard Oil of California (later ARAMCO) obtains a 60-year concession to explore for oil in Saudi territory.
1945:	Abd al-Aziz ibn Saud meets with President Franklin Roosevelt of the United States.
1951:	Saudi Arabia and the United States sign a treaty of assistance and mutual defense.
1953:	In November King Abd-al-Aziz ibn Saud dies and is succeeded by the

Crown Prince, Saud bin Abd al-Aziz al-Saud. The new king's brother, Faisal, is named Crown Prince.

1960: The Organization of Petroleum Exporting Countries (OPEC) is created by the governments of Iran, Iraq, Kuwait, Saudi Arabia, and Venezuela.

1961: Kuwait obtains independence from Great Britain.

1970: The war in North Yemen ends with an agreement between Saudi Arabia and Yemen.

1971: Britain withdraws from the Gulf. Bahrain, Qatar, and the Trucial States gain independence. The Trucial States band together to form the United Arab Emirates.

1973: Reacting to U.S. support for Israel in the 1973 Arab-Israeli war, Saudi Arabia and other Gulf countries cut oil production and impose a short-lived oil embargo on the United States.

1975: In March Saudi King Faisal is assassinated. Khalid is proclaimed king.

1979: Juhaiman al-Utaibi and his band of armed zealots take over the Grand Mosque in Mecca. Toward the end of the year, there is a Shiite uprising in the country's eastern province. Saudi Arabia severs diplomatic relations with Egypt after it makes peace with Israel.

1981: The Gulf Cooperation Council is created.

1982: King Khalid dies and is succeeded by his brother, Fahd.

1988: Saudi Arabia nationalizes ARAMCO.

1990: Iraq invades Kuwait in August; in response, the United States sends troops to protect Saudi Arabia and begins organizing a coalition to oppose the Iraqi aggression. Unification takes place in Yemen.

1991: The Gulf War is launched from bases in Saudi Arabia, and coalition forces drive the Iraqi army out of Kuwait. Saudi Islamists led by Safar al-Hawali petition King Fahd for reforms, but are rebuffed.

1992: In March King Fahd approves the creation of a consultative assembly for Saudi Arabia.

1995: King Fahd suffers a stroke, and Crown Prince Abdullah assumes control of the government.

2001: On September 11 al-Qaeda attacks the United States. Fifteen of the 19 hijackers involved in attacks on New York and Washington are Saudi nationals. As a result, relations between the United States and Saudi Arabia cool. King Fahd calls for the eradication of terrorism, saying it is prohibited by Islam.

2002: The Saudi foreign minister says his country will not allow the United States to use its facilities to attack Iraq, even in a UN-sanctioned strike.

2003: In March the United States and a handful of allies attack Iraq, quickly defeating the Iraqi army and toppling the government of Saddam Hussein. In April the United States announces that it will pull out almost all its troops from Saudi Arabia, ending a military presence dating back to the 1991 Persian Gulf War. Both countries stress that they will remain allies.

2005: King Fahd dies on August 1, and is succeeded by Abdullah.

2007: In April Saudi police arrest 172 people suspected of terrorist activities.

ARAMCO—The national oil company of Saudi Arabia, which is headquartered in Dhahran. ARAMCO was originally an American-owned company called the Arabian-American Oil Company. The government of Saudi Arabia gained control of ARAMCO between 1973 and 1980.

emir—an Arabic term meaning "prince" or "commander." In the Arabian Peninsula the word is used to denote the rulers of several of the Persian Gulf states, including Kuwait, Bahrain, Qatar, and the seven states of the United Arab Emirates. The territory governed by an emir is known as an emirate.

Hashemite—a descendant of Hashim, the great-grandfather of the Prophet Muhammad. After World War I, the Allies placed Hashemites on the thrones of Iraq, Syria, the Hejaz, and Jordan; today, Jordan is the only state with a Hashemite ruler.

Hejaz—a region in northwestern Saudi Arabia. Its principal city is Jedda, but the region also contains the Islamic holy cities of Mecca and Medina.

Ikhwan—the religious militia that comprised the military force of Abd al-Aziz ibn Saud, the founder of Saudi Arabia. The Ikhwan were made up of Bedouin. Following Abd al-Aziz's conquest of the Hejaz in 1926, elements of the Ikhwan challenged the king but were defeated by Abd al-Aziz in 1929.

imam—usually a prayer leader, but this term can also be used to refer to the leader of a Muslim community. Shiite Muslims use the term to refer to divinely inspired descendants of the Prophet Muhammad.

Nejd—literally, "highland" in Arabic, a name for central Arabia. The Saudi royal family originated in Nejd, and Riyadh, the capital of Saudi Arabia, is located there.

Rashidis—the Rashidis were a dynasty of rulers belonging to the Shammar tribe, which ruled Nejd following the destruction of the first Saudi state in 1818 by the

Ottomans. The Rashidi capital was Hail. The Rashidis cooperated with the Ottomans and were decisively defeated by Abd al-Aziz ibn Saud in 1921.

sheikh——an Arabic word that literally means "elder," and is applied to revered figures such as tribal leaders, Islamic scholars, or wise men.

Shia——The second-largest sect in Islam. In contrast to the Sunnis, the Shia believe that legitimate leadership of the Islamic community must remain in the family of the Prophet Muhammad. In the Arabian Peninsula, Shiites are found in eastern Saudi Arabia, Kuwait, Bahrain, and Yemen.

Sunni——the largest sectarian grouping in Islam. The word comes from *sunna*, an Arabic term that means "the path" and refers to the example set the Prophet Muhammad and his companions, which Muslims are expected to emulate.

Trucial States——a name given collectively to a number of small emirates and principalities along the Gulf coast of the Arabian Peninsula, in reference to the long-running treaties between Great Britain and the local Arab sheikhs. Most of the Trucial States (the emirates of Abu Dhabi, Ajman, Dubai, Fujairah, Ras al-Khaimah, Sharjah, and Umm al-Quwain) formed the United Arab Emirates in 1971, while Bahrain opted for separate independence.

ulama——Muslim religious scholars, who typically have completed a course of Islamic studies at a *madrassa* (Islamic school).

Wahhabi——Western name for the puritanical Muslim sect that derives its teachings from the medieval jurist Ahmed ibn Hanbal. The sect was established in Arabia during the 18th century by Muhammad ibn Abd al-Wahhab, and is now the dominant version of Islam in Saudi Arabia, Qatar, and other Gulf states.

Aburish, Said. *The Rise, Corruption and Coming Fall of the House of Saud.* New York: Palgrave/Macmillan, 1996.

Commins, David. *The Wahhabi Mission and Saudi Arabia.* London: I.B. Tauris, 2006.

Davidson, Christopher. *The United Arab Emirates: A Study in Survival.* Boulder: Lynne Rienner, 2005.

Delong-Bas, Natana. *Wahhabi Islam: From Revival and Reform to Jihad.* Cambridge: Oxford University Press, 2004.

Fandy, Mamoun. *Saudi Arabia and the Politics of Dissent.* New York: St. Martin's Press, 1999.

Kelly, J.B. *Arabia, The Gulf, and the West.* New York: Basic Books, 1981.

Kostiner, Joseph. *The Making of Saudi Arabia, 1916–1936.* Oxford: Oxford University Press, 1993.

Al-Rasheed, Madawi. *A History of Saudi Arabia.* Cambridge: Cambridge University Press, 2002.

Al-Rasheed, Madawi. *Contesting the Saudi State: Islamic Voices from a New Generation.* Cambridge: Cambridge University Press, 2007.

Vassiliev, Alexei. *The History of Saudi Arabia.* New York: New York University Press, 2000.

Wynbrandt, James. *A Brief History of Saudi Arabia.* New York: Checkmark Books, 2004.

http://www.saudi-us-relations.org/

An independent, private-sector information resource that offers objective, comprehensive news and information on the history, breadth, and depth of the relationship between the United States and Saudi Arabia.

http://www.arab.net/

A collection of articles written by leading journalists and editors in the Middle East. It provides coverage of the states of the Arabian Peninsula.

https://www.cia.gov/cia/publications/factbook/index.html

The CIA World Factbook contains updated factual information on Saudi Arabia and other Arabian counties.

http://www.shura.gov.sa/EnglishSite/EIndex.htm

Official site of the Majlis al-Shura, Saudi Arabia's consultative council, formed by King Fahd in 1992. It includes the laws and by-laws of the council, as well as the curriculum vitae of each member of the council (in Arabic and English).

http://www.saudia-online.com/

A portal site on social, economic, and political aspects of Saudi society.

http://www.sauditimes.com

English language online newspaper with up-to-date political and economic information on Saudi Arabia.

Numbers in **bold italic** refer to captions.

Contributors

John Calvert is Associate Professor of History at Creighton University in Omaha, Nebraska, where he teaches courses related to the medieval and modern periods of Middle East history. He received his Ph.D. degree from McGill University's Institute of Islamic Studies in Montreal in 1994. With William Shepard he is editor, translator, and author of *Sayyid Qutb A Child from the Village* (Syracuse University Press, 2004). He edited a special issue of the journal *Historical Reflections/Reflexions Historiques* entitled "Islam and Modernity," and is the author of a number of articles and chapters dealing with modern Islamic thinkers and movements. Dr. Calvert is currently working on a reference and source guide on Islamism.

Picture Credits